My modules,
Your wealth

Richard Schleinkofer

DEDICATION

To all human beings having a willing to change

FOREWORD

Dear Reader

With this book, I would like to introduce you to the connection between spiritual thinking and personal wealth. Wealth refers on the one hand to personality development but also to material richness, which almost inevitably arises from it. In our common time of life, in which work compression, information overflow, hecticness and thus stress determine our life, everyone should develop strategies for himself, in order to focus on the most important things from his personal point of view. I have done this for myself with this book, among others, and would like to share it with others.

The interpretation of terms or necessary questions in the respective chapters I have developed partly by reading numerous spiritual books. The connection to wealth I make from economic books and my personal experience, which I have collected in a decades-long economic life.

In order to become personally and materially rich, eight topics are of extraordinary relevance to me:

- Letting go
- Self-love
- Living Consciousness
- Accept - Change - Leave
- Fearlessness
- Setting goals
- Copying Patterns
- Feeling security.

To help you navigate through these eight thematic chapters, I have divided each chapter into five basic questions (each slightly modified):

1.) What is the meaning?
2.) How do you achieve it?
3.) Why does it strengthen the personality?
4.) How does this contribute to my wealth?
5.) What are the idioms on the subject?

In the context of the first (meaning) question, I concentrate on the essentials. You may save yourself the reading of many books. The answer to the second question (How do I achieve this?) gives you hints for the implementation/solution of the problem described by me for the respective topics. Questions three and four show you the consequences: Ways to the personality development and to your personal wealth. The re-interpretations selected by me do not only round off the respective chapter, but also give a very good insight into how mankind or personalities of contemporary history, partly for centuries, think about the respective topic.

After the eight thematic chapters, I try to give you practical implementation tips via summaries and success formulas. I hope these will help you.

Dear reader, in this book you will be asked many questions. This is to set necessary thinking processes with you in motion. Of course, it is also not useless, since you can restructure and align yourself by writing such a guidebook.

By the way, my personal goal is no longer monetary wealth, but rather to go through life much more relaxed and "cooler". Achieving that is my personal aspired wealth. I hope my book helps you find your personal wealth.
I will give investment recommendations for ETF's (Exchange Traded Funds) in the first eight chapters. Due to the market situation and the real estate prices at the beginning of the 2020's, this form of investment seems to me to make the most sense now.

I wish you a lot of fun while reading and an impulse for changes in your life!

My modules, Your wealth

CONTENTS

ACKNOWLEDGMENTS

FOREWORD

AFTERWORD

ACKNOWLEDGMENTS

Thanks to my wife for the inspiration

1 LETTING GO

> Serenity means letting go of the past and the future
> and releasing fears.
> (Ebo Rau (*1945), German physician)

1.1 What does letting go mean?

Letting go is the opposite of holding on. Many people are convinced that they can let go, but in reality they only repress.

> ➤ **Letting go is the ability not to cling to something or someone.**

The most important prerequisite for letting go is the prior (unconditional) acceptance of a person/thing. For example, if you have not accepted someone as he/she is, it is difficult to let go of that person. It can also be that something material is attached to you (unconsciously), of which you are not yet fully aware that you can or even must let go of it.

Possibly a certain possession, a social position or a job is attached to you, through which you unconsciously hope for recognition. This can also happen to you through your life partner and your family, so that you feel "attached" to these persons or even define yourself through them. These are basically your backpacks that you carry with you in terms of your personality.

However, in order to become inwardly free, you should first detach yourself from them in a mental game and analyze what remains (of you) and how you define (or see) yourself today as a person - without the mentioned backpacks. What remains of you then? Through this book you will come closer to answering this question. Letting go is therefore also a basic prerequisite for recognizing who you actually are.

1.2 How do I achieve letting go?

If you realize, for example, that you define yourself through material things (e.g. house, apartment, car, etc.) or your status (e.g. job, position in the company, etc.), you are already on the right path. However, think intensively about how such topics and things dominate your life. Do you still determine your life yourself or are you determined by the material?

Of course, letting go does not mean that you should or must separate from your family, your wife, your husband, your job or the like. Nevertheless, you should critically question your private and professional (environmental) attachments with regard to your own existence. With such reflections, you will possibly find out what else is attached to you besides the examples I mentioned.

From whom or what can you let go?

- For example, negative feelings and prejudices that you may have towards colleagues at work, your boss, strangers, etc. Where do these actually come from? Analyzing this requires an individual in-depth analysis, which I can unfortunately only give you in part in this book, since I am not a trained psychologist and do not know your individual situation. However, to bring the whole thing to a common denominator: You should first forgive yourself for these negative feelings, this is the fastest way to let go of them.

- Where does your inner desire for reward and recognition come from that you carry around inside? Probably you (like most people) were brought up in a reward/ punishment system. Of course, as a child, you liked reward and recognition much better than punishment and blame. Nevertheless, your upbringing is long gone. You should develop your own inner frame of reference that makes you independent of external recognition. Are you dependent on recognition from others? No, because you know that you are good enough for yourself. So let go of the desire for reward and recognition. Acknowledge and praise yourself; you are your best man or woman. Build your own inner frame of reference. By this, I mean the creation of your own value scheme.

- Who actually defines what success and what failure is? You do everything as well as you can and according to your best knowledge and conscience. (That is what your parents did, by the way; believe it or not). An alien/strange definition for success or failure has been drummed into you. Try to find your own definition of success and let it apply to you. Let go of foreign ideas and definitions of success or failure.

- Do not think that you are always the master in your house. Your personal universe is determined by many factors and therefore you cannot influence everything in your environment. Let go of the idea that you are or must always be the doer.

- Forgive yourself for your views, thoughts and actions of yesterday, if they were questionable from today's point of view. You do not necessarily have to regret them. However, you have the chance to start anew every day. Let go now of your views, thoughts and deeds that may be in need of renovation.

You may think that the above examples and topics are a good illustration of exactly who or what you can let go of. Nevertheless, how does letting go work in practice? Is there perhaps a manual for this?

Unfortunately, there is no generally binding solution, because we humans are too individual and everyone carries his or her own story. From my personal point of view, however, I can name five steps that you can generally take in order to let go in a targeted way:

1.) First, it is essential and indispensable to realize the burden by holding on (or not letting go) to material things or persons. This can arise, in which one - possibly unconsciously - builds up resistance against an existing reality, does not accept topics or situations properly in the first place, or through the fear of the uncertainty of life, which one carries with oneself.

Some people, for example, simply do not want to acknowledge that their partner has fallen out of love and separated. Nevertheless, they cling to this love for a long time, because they do not want to come to terms with being alone and do not want to let the former companion move on in peace. Thus, people who act accordingly find no other way to deal with their loss and therefore hold on to what they are used to.

Others see their economic future as anything but rosy. So they start to accumulate and hoard material things in their household. This can be clothes, which one never carried and this also very probably never will do, in addition, discarded furniture, which one can use - so the thought - perhaps again sometime in the distant future. Closets or cellar compartments are then unnecessarily converted into storage facilities.

Both examples illustrate that holding on to feelings or material things inevitably becomes a burden. Inside, the energy can no longer flow freely.

2.) The next step is the removal of the often unconscious and deep-seated fear and the thereby established resistances. You should weigh well the possible consequences of letting go. Be aware of the freedom ahead of you that will be achieved by letting go of the emotional ballast inside you and weigh the consequences of holding on to old thought patterns. In chapter five I will describe in more detail how you can counter the fear of emerging uncertainty and insecurity.

To come back to the two examples above, there are clear reasons for letting go. On the other hand, there are borderline cases for which you should first decide whether a letting go question arises at all.

Maybe you are the one who has fallen out of love, but you are not sure if it is really so? Maybe you have lost part of your self-love, lost connection to your feelings, or are holding on to wishful thinking and projecting that onto your relationship? The next chapter may show you how to regain self-love.

3.) As a third step, it is advisable to mentally imagine the relief by letting go. What would it be like if tomorrow you could live without this burden? You might have more time for yourself and your thoughts, definitely more space in your closet and your basement, but most of all more freedom to find and realize yourself.

4.) After an inner discussion of the issue to be let go of (weighing the pro's and con's of the issue), a decision should be made for or against letting   go.
With material things, the consideration is certainly easier to accomplish than with thoughts or feelings. For the former, there are interesting books that can support you (e.g. "Feng Shui - Against the clutter of everyday life") or methods such as those of Marie Kondo: Take each item in your hand; if it triggers a spark of joy in you and you can use it

in everyday life, keep it. If it does not, say goodbye to that item in gratitude.

With thoughts/feelings or relationship topics the weighing is already clearly more difficult, because possibly dependencies can block a discussion or the common built up is glorified too strongly. These dependencies can be of a personal nature (there are children together) but also of a financial nature (one is the main breadwinner of the joint household).

5.) After a decision for letting go, the basic readiness and acceptance for it should be established comprehensively. Only then can implementation take place and attachments be consciously released. Establishing or ensuring acceptance is perhaps the most difficult of these five steps. Often one establishes only a superficial acceptance, because one does not yet want to perceive the result of one's own inner discussion. However, you can only achieve the implementation if you reach/ensure the full acceptance of your own decision. To be able to let go means first to trust yourself.

This also frees you from the fear of possibly making the wrong decision. In case of doubt, a "no" made out of intuition as an answer to a decisive question is always to be evaluated as more meaningful and more accurate than a "yes", which is made after eternal back and forth thinking.

By the way, you can also ritualize the act of

letting go (e.g. by burning records of your deliberations, pictures or similar). This has helped many people in this process.

1.3 Why does letting go strengthen my personality?

Letting go is an important prerequisite for surrender and achieving personal freedom. It can help you to become more serene and balanced.

Letting go creates lightness, peace as well as joy and thus leads to abundance, because you finally recognize the important things/characteristics in you that you already carry within you today. In addition, you do not harm yourself, because you close with burdensome topics from the past. This also leads to a certain looseness and thus to balance and calmness.

What opinion have you actually formed about yourself? Think about it and ... just let it be in the future! You do not have to form an opinion about yourself. You have the right just to be there and to exist!

You have been suggested a certain value scheme as a child over the upbringing, school and education, which determines your thinking and acting until today. Who says then that this value scheme is so correct? It is relative, because it was evaluated with the standards of others. Moreover, you have taken it over (possibly without questioning it)! If you had grown up in another environment, in another family or in another country, you would certainly have developed another value scheme. Consequently, you may be prejudiced against other views, actions and people you meet. Stop it! Reconsider your bias!

Inwardly, you make almost all of your decisions from a certain security aspect. Once you have understood that security, as you define it for yourself, may not exist, you live more liberated and courageous. Because only one thing is certain: you will die one day. Therefore, decide to live free.

Why do you take part in the comparative race for power, possessions and wealth with your friends, neighbors and work colleagues? This can cost you quality of life and above all valuable lifetime - especially through the constant comparison with others. Let go of your ambition if it is comparatively motivated!

By the way, the saying (which was used for propaganda purposes in the time of National Socialism, among others): "Who fights can lose, who does not fight, has already lost" is from my point of view fundamentally wrong. From my point of view, it is true: Who fights wastes energy. You can use this energy better for yourself.

1.4 How does letting go contribute to my wealth?

Victim or martyr roles or imposed views and perpetrator roles that may have been suggested to you in childhood keep you from positive success thinking. If you let go of such attachments that keep you from a clear and positive direction, you can use the energy and time you gain for yourself even better.

You can use these resources to develop your personal formula for success. Ask yourself what your strengths are, what you are good at, what you have done well in the last few years? Write this down once and find out what you particularly enjoyed doing. This can be the beginning of your career. Here slumbers the potential to your wealth, which you should raise.

Time is money. What does this mean in the context of letting go? Quite simply, the time gained by letting go of secondary issues gives you the opportunity to focus more on the issues that are really close to your heart. For example, before investing time or money, you can better discuss your real concerns. I will go into more detail about secondary issues in Chapter 13.

Can you develop wealth by letting go? Isn't that a contradiction? No, it is absolutely not a contradiction. Besides the resource, gains in time and energy already mentioned above, there are much more concrete examples:

Let us assume you have a stock portfolio that contains several stocks. Unfortunately, all stocks seldom perform equally well and so it can happen that you hold positions in your portfolio that have developed negatively. However, as part of your personal portfolio management, it is difficult to let go of these stocks. The reasons for not letting go can be of different nature: It might be shares of the company where you work, you have inherited them and therefore have a personal connection to these stocks or you believe that the stocks will recover and you just have to be patient. Most of the time you wait for years for a price recovery and a turn for the better does not happen.

If you get out of such stocks in time (even at a loss) - i.e. let go - and invest in more promising stocks, you can make the money work much better for you.

Here are my ETF buying recommendations for "letting-goers". I am assuming you are not invested in ETF's yet. Therefore I advise you to buy the following: Black Rock's MSCI World with the security identification number (WKN) or International Security Identification Number (ISIN): IE00B4L5Y983. This is a passive accumulating fund, i.e. the profits are reinvested. The fund volume is very large with more than 40 billion euros (probably one of the largest ETF in the world) and the costs are very favorable with 0.20% per year. There are more than 1,600 individual stocks of the world included in this ETF.

The MSCI World is also available in a distributing variant. For example, the issuer DWS with the ISIN: IE00BK1PV551 gives out an inexpensive version (0.19%).

1.5 What are the idioms about letting go?

The idioms on the subject of letting go show one thing above all: It is obviously a difficult subject. First two examples, to which I give my opinion in the following:

With every letting go, we also give away a piece of ourselves... (Elvira von Ostheim).

What one has, one should not let go, as long as one has nothing else (author unknown).

The author of the first statement (1) claims that with every letting go one gives away a piece of oneself. I see this to one hundred and eighty degrees differently: with each letting go, we rather go a piece towards our real self, since we - as described above - were very strongly formed by others in our life (through education, school, etc.). Each letting go of these imposed/acquired backpacks brings us closer to ourselves. We may give away something of our previous self - we unburden ourselves and expose our real self.

The second statement (2) is also doubtful or at least questionable for me: As long as you cannot let go of your deeply internalized habits, you will not be able to open the door to the new in your life.

Here are a few examples that can help you let go:

1.) Get rid of the idea that your happiness depends on something outside yourself (Neale Donald Walsch).

2.) A common misconception in Zen teaching is that we have to "let go. We cannot force ourselves to "let go." We must perceive the underlying fear (Charlotte Joko Beck).

3.) It is strange that even when we let go we still think that we have to do something (Helga Schäferling).

4.) When I let go of what I am, I become what I could be. When I let go of what I have, I get what I need (Lao-tzu).

The third example describes one thing very well: Only you are responsible for your happiness and no one else! I hope you are aware of your responsibility for yourself. You cannot become fundamentally happier if you suddenly had more money (the lottery win excuse) or a better professional position. You can only achieve your happiness yourself through your inner positioning.

The fourth example describes an important connection: If you have difficulties with letting go, there is some fear behind it, which you may not be aware of yet. This was also the reason why I included the topic of fear in the book. Often it is the fear of indeterminacy (also uncertainty, insecurity), which I will come back to later in the book. We would like to know beforehand what will happen if we let go of one thing or another....

The fifth example is a pointer to our performance society. Even with the topic of letting go, which should actually be easy for us, we see considerable efforts connected. Maybe because it is not so easy for us?

My modules, Your wealth

2. SELF-LOVE

> Self-love is the strongest, most sacred bond
> that unites and holds us together with humanity.
> (Heinrich Martin (1818 - 1872), German writer)

2.1 What does self-love mean?

Self-love should not be confused with narcissism or egoism. Narcissism is rather self-love, which goes so far that one considers oneself more important or more valuable than others and therefore pays less attention to others. In contrast, egoism is rather self-interest, which goes so far that one's actions serve only one's own advantage.

> ➢ **Self-love is the comprehensive acceptance of oneself through unrestricted love for oneself.**

According to the Greek doctrine of mesotes (Greek: middle; position of a virtue between two opposing vices, e.g., excess and deficiency), self-love/self-acceptance stands in the middle between egoism/selfishness and self-denial (denial of one's own desires and feelings in favor of someone or something else). In this middle of the opposite "virtues", selfishness and self-denial are then also other characteristics such as self-respect, self-trust, self-devotion and self-esteem.

Can you say about yourself that you love yourself? Why is this so difficult for you? You probably were not raised that way... It begs the question, what would an education in self-love look like? This topic would be worth a whole book of its own.

2.2 How do I achieve self-love?

It is sometimes so simple: treat, speak and think about yourself as you would someone you really love.

Love yourself now, today and from now on always and do not wait until someone else does it, maybe you feel better or changes occur in your life. Start now and do your best!

Accept yourself and acknowledge yourself. Do not criticize yourself. If you criticize yourself, you undermine yourself. Criticizing yourself changes nothing. When you acknowledge yourself, you strengthen yourself. Accept yourself for who you are.

Here are a few thoughts, helps and affirmations that support achieving self- love:

- I am good the way I am and find only good things about myself.

- I am grateful for the fact that I can be in the world for the period of a lifetime. This gives me satisfaction because I can change something for the better during this time.

- I never harm myself and think rightly of myself.

- I forgive myself and let go of the past. I have done the best I could so far with the understanding, attention and knowledge that was available to me at the time.

- I do not scare myself and am kind to my thoughts.

- I praise myself. Praise builds me up. I praise myself as often as I can. I praise myself for every little thing I do well. I also praise others as often as I can.

- I give myself support. I find ways to support myself.

- I have fun. I remember the things that brought me joy in the past. I incorporate them into my life. I figure out how to have fun with everything I do.

- I work out my successes and make them clear to myself. I strengthen my strengths and stop comparing.

- I find out what success is for me.

In addition, very important: I do it now! Postscript: Always remember: you are the main character in your life.

2.3 Why does self-love strengthen my personality?

By fully accepting yourself (self-love), you simultaneously strengthen all other virtues that are in the environment of self-love.

You additionally strengthen your self-confidence and self-awareness. You reflect yourself positively. Furthermore, your self-esteem increases. The strengthening of these virtues is also an important prerequisite for an increased body awareness and a sensible diet. In addition, you will find it easier to determine your personal location.

2.4 How does self-love contribute to my wealth?

You become more confident in your decisions and know in which direction you want to go. You do not hold on to nonsensical things or investments for nostalgic reasons. You become more positively selfish and ask yourself more often "What do I get out of it?".

You subliminally align your activities, investments and commitment to a (your) definition and calculation of success and thus avoid "hobbyism" (nonsensical commitments/investments out of attachment, nostalgia or familiarity). You know what you want.

Your individual strategy can arise from your "clarity of direction". You know where and how you want to invest or get personally involved; in terms of both money and time.

Do you know in which direction you want to go with your investments? Do you plan to invest in real estate, shares, funds, ETF's and how do you want to realize them? Through savings plans, one-time investments, other asset accumulation? What risks are you willing to take? Maybe you want to relax and let your money work for you and take care of other issues?

Here are my ETF purchase recommendations for self-lovers. I advise you to buy the following: The MSCI EM (=Emerging Markets) from Amundi with the security identification number (WKN) or International Security Identification Number (ISIN): LU1681045370. This is a passive reinvesting fund, i.e. the profits are reinvested. The fund volume is large with more than 3 billion euros (in principle, a fund volume of more than 1 billion is considered large). The costs are very favorable with 0.20% per year. You invest here in emerging markets.

The MSCI EM is also available in a distributing version. The publisher Black Rock, for example, issues a low-cost version with ISIN IE00B0M63177 (0.18% per year).

2.5 Which sayings are there on the subject of self-love?

During my research for significant sayings, aphorisms and proverbs on the subject of self-love, one fact in particular caught my eye: There are many derogatory, warning and reprimanding statements and proverbs on this topic. By the way, this already starts in the Bible and in Greek mythology and continues up to the present. Here first, some (from my view) negative examples:

1.) Self-love is a wind-filled hose, from which storms escape, if one stabs into it even with a needle (Voltaire).

2.) It is dull to be able to honor nothing but oneself (Friedrich Hebbel).

3.) Self-love is one of the greatest diseases that we bring into the world. It is blind like love (for a beautiful woman). He who does not temper it cannot become a great man. The ignorant man seems to be wise and commits a thousand inevitable mistakes (Wilhelm Heinse).

4.)   What is more foolish than to be charmed by one's own good qualities, to be enraptured by one's own merits (Erasmus of Rotterdam)?

5.)   Self-love is above all the mother of self-deception and self-conceit (Heribert Rau).

6.)   Self-love is the tool of our self-preservation; it has much in common with the tool of our propagation: it is necessary, it is dear to us, it gives us pleasure, and it must be concealed (Voltaire).

I think Voltaire rather wanted to address the ego in example 1. In people who have a big ego, storms are indeed ignited when it is poked at. Self-love is not filled with wind, but with clarity about oneself. Rather, it is the basis for a person to be able to give and love at all.

In my view, honoring oneself is not dull at all (2). Rather, we have forgotten how to honor ourselves. In addition, who can still honor father and mother today? Accepting ourselves, honoring ourselves, and reflecting on ourselves through introspection is incredibly important to creating a fulfilling life.

Why should we moderate our self-love (example 3)? What does it mean to be a great man/human being? We in no way appear wise through self-love as described in the example, nor do we commit mistakes. What mistakes should these be? Only those who love themselves get to know themselves and can find out whom they are.

It is not foolish to be delighted with yourself (4)! Moreover, of course you can be proud of yourself.

What is there to be self-deception about self-love (5)? This example clearly underlines how the literature warns against self-love.

The last idiom is actually another good one (6). In this one it is described that self-love (according to Voltaire) must be hidden. Why is this so in our society? Possibly because self-love is confused with narcissism?

In the following, I have now compiled a few positive

examples, which in principle represent exactly the opposite of the phrases listed above:

7.) Self-love is the source, the origin and the principle of all our passions; it alone arises with man and never leaves him as long as he lives (Jean-Jacques Rousseau).

8.) Most people do not perish from life, but from an unhappy love - for themselves (Gerhard Uhlenbruck).

9.) You can give love to yourself; surely, you are loved in this way. There is no one who in life so much real love (Friedrich Löchner).

10.) May we have self-love? Certainly! It only depends on who it is that we love (Johann Jakob Mohr).

11.) We do not have enough self-love to despise the contempt with which others regard us (Luc de Clapiers).

12.) All love in this world is built on self-love. If you left self-love, you would easily leave the whole world (Meister Eckhart).

13.) The love that each one has for himself is not accidental, but a feeling planted in him by nature (Aristotle).

14.) Self-love makes us completely what we are (Claude-Adrien Helvetius).

15.) In the love to ourselves lies the secret of a fulfilled life (Gudrun Kropp).

Self-love is one of the greatest sources of your personal energy. Only if you carry this in you, you can also give love. The people, who lose it, certainly lose their love of life (7, 8).

The poem under (9) shows once again very beautifully that you should and can love yourself sincerely.

In (10), the question is asked whether we know who we actually are. However, even if we do not know that yet, we can still develop self-love. I think self-love is the basis for finding out who we are.

The important proverb in (11) wants to tell us that if we have enough self-love, any disrespect of others cannot affect us at all. Negative as well as positive judgments should not affect us at all. To go deeper into this topic, I would like to recommend the book "The Four Promises" by Don Manuel Ruiz. In the chapter "Don't take anything personally", it is very well described how to deal with personal praise or blame.

Meister Eckhart, who lived from 1260 - 1327, knew early on what is essential. Self-love is the basis of love (12).

Every human being has received a portion of self-love from birth. Unfortunately, in the course of their lives, many people forget how important it is and instead take on a victim role (13).

In my view, nothing needs to be added to the last two sayings (14, 15), since they speak for themselves (the secret of a fulfilled life).

3. LIVE CONSCIOUSNESS

Our consciousness decides whether possibility becomes reality.
(Kersten Kämpfer (*1958), Dr.-Ing. of Technical Cybernetics)

3.1 What does consciousness mean?

The opposite of consciousness is unawareness or even unconsciousness. Many people believe that they live and think consciously. Instead, they are controlled by their mind, which is constantly talking to itself, and thus think or act unconsciously.

> ➤ **Consciousness is the actual experience of mental states of knowledge.**

Consciousness has incredibly many and different definitions. Depending on the point of view from which one approaches this great subject (religion, natural science, philosophy, psychology, etc.).

From my point of view, the most important definitions for the purpose of this book are the following distinctions:

- The consciousness that has control over thoughts, decisions and coordination is called access consciousness.

- Those who think, remember, plan, and expect have thoughtful consciousness.

- Conscious experience and thinking are separable.

Fatally, our mind - actually permanently - controls our mental consciousness, so that we constantly think about the past or worry about the future, forgetting to perceive the moment and ourselves in it. Furthermore, we want to get things as perfect as possible (in the future) by planning future scenarios and thereby put ourselves under massive stress.

In addition, by dwelling on past situations, we fuel our guilty conscience, which often leads to sadness, because we believe that we could have done many things better or differently. This is unnecessary and pointless, because the past is unchangeable and will always remain so. Only our attitude to it is changeable, thus also the memory of certain events.

3.2 How do I achieve consciousness?

Both mind-driven ways of thinking - future consciousness and past consciousness (mental consciousness) lead to an unconscious life, because we constantly derive thoughts about our past (and almost continuously wallow in the past) or project ideas into the future. We perceive the current daily life partly only as in trance - thus unconsciously.

For me it is crucial to regain the access consciousness, i.e. the control over thoughts, decisions and coordination, and thereby to push back the mind (the mental consciousness) which is constantly speaking to itself, or even to bring it to zero.

This can only be achieved by persistent observation of one's own world of thoughts. The permanent question is the following: Is one just present or lost in the past/future world? Furthermore, the focus must be put on the perception of acute situations. These sensory perceptions should be done without evaluation; otherwise, there is the danger of a relapse into the mode of perception of the mind. Meditations and affirmations can help with this.

I have listed here three excellent works on the subject of consciousness (subjectively, based on the books I have read so far):

- Eckhart Tolle: A New Earth - Leap of Consciousness instead of Self-Destruction

- Harald Wessbecher: Unfold your destiny - live the way it suits and pleases you

- Osho: Consciousness - Observe without judging.

3.3 Why does consciousness strengthen my personality?

Living in full consciousness leads to a great personal awareness and presentness. One experiences one's life more intensively and it is additionally decelerated in time. You prolong your actively lived life time, also because you do not constantly (mentally) rehash past topics and experience them again by mentally retrieving them.

One simply lives in the here and now or strikingly: One is in the middle of it instead of just being there.

Through the full existence, you should have only little time to think about past or future.

3.4 How does consciousness contribute to my wealth?

You are fully present in all kinds of conversations. Whether in conversations with partners, friends, bankers, insurance agents, teachers, superiors, or wealth managers. You listen well. You do not let yourself be blinded or sold hopes. You do not let yourself be put off - not even by your boss. You develop your personal compass that tells you what is right.

Your presence and your active listening are highly appreciated by your interlocutors and valued accordingly.

According to my observations, many people are not even aware of the insanity they engage in when doing private business. They drive kilometers to distant discounters because, for example, strawberries are fifty cents cheaper there. If it concerns however a house and/or a dwelling purchase - possibly over several hundred thousand euro - the bank and real estate advisor will already make everything correct (similar applies with car purchases). However, if you are fully aware of what you are doing, what impact your actions may have, you will certainly shift your prioritization and attention accordingly. By the way, relatively little will happen if you buy the strawberries 50 cents more expensive...

The wealth formula here is relatively simple: big deals have a big impact, small deals have a small impact; be aware of that. So be very aware especially of the big deals. Aside from the time, you will save if you stop looking for the benefits of small deals...

With an increased presentness, you simply notice trends more promptly, since you no longer wallow in future or past topics. Have you noticed, for example, that people are investing in individual stocks in a much more sophisticated way than in ETFs (Exchange Traded Funds)? These are exchange-traded index funds with the help of which you can build up assets in the long term with shares. Stock lists are reproduced or sector pools are compiled, such as the DAX, Standard & Poor's 500 or the world stock index MSCI World. The return results from the mass of individual shares. A major advantage of these baskets is that fluctuations (both upward and downward) are not as significant, i.e., if an individual stock performs poorly, it does not immediately drag down your portfolio. An ETF is just as safe as an actively managed fund and is protected accordingly in case of bankruptcy of the issuer. Since ETF's are passive funds, the fees are also much lower than actively managed funds.

Are you following what is going on in the cryptocurrencies space right now? Yes, I admit that the topic is very new and correspondingly risky. However, it is certain for me that the topic will come and you should be there at the right time.

Here are my ETF purchase recommendations for awareness living ones. I advise the following purchases: State Street's MSCI All Country World with the security identification number (WKN) or International Security Identification Number (ISIN): IE00B44Z5B48. This is a passive accumulating fund, i.e. the profits are reinvested. The fund volume is large with more than 3 billion euros. The costs are favorable at 0.40% per year. In principle, this ETF is a mix of the MSCI World plus stocks from developing emerging markets.

The MSCI All Country World is also available in a distributing version. The publisher Vanguard, for example, issues a low-cost version with ISIN: IE00B3RBWM25 (0.22% per year).

3.5 What idioms are there on the subject of living consciousness?

Expressions about consciousness often have positive connotations. Obviously, many people find it desirable to live consciously without knowing exactly what that actually is. I have chosen four phrases below to show you the benefits of living consciously:

1.) The state, the nature of consciousness is, with regard to the happiness of our existence, the main thing. For consciousness alone is the immediate, everything else is indirect, through and in it. Since our life is not, like that of the plant, an unconscious one, but a conscious one, and therefore has a consciousness as its basis and universal condition, the quality and degree of perfection of this consciousness is obviously the most essential thing for a pleasant or unpleasant life (Arthur Schopenhauer).

2.) Our consciousness transforms infinite possibilities into reality (Kersten Kämpfer).

3.) Life is the conscious perception of the moment (Irina Rauthmann).

4.) What does not become consciousness is not lived (Friedrich Löchner).

To call consciousness Schopenhauer has already formulated the immediate aptly in a few lines by the simplicity of the explanation (example 1). However, even much better: To explain the nature and the degree of perfection of consciousness, as the most essential thing to a pleasant or unpleasant life is downright ingenious. You should take this as an incentive to work on your consciousness.

If you do not live in the past or in the future, in the moment of the moment, the possibilities and chances become apparent to you, which you only have to take up. This is excellently described in the second and third examples.

The last example is from my point of view also by the shortness a very memorable one. Surely, you have experienced people on vacation who really film everything. Even the buffet is not spared.

Do these people live in the here and now? One can have justified doubts about this. Do these people consciously perceive their vacation through the lens of their camera? Probably not, because they have to try to find a suitable angle when photographing and filming. Only what you perceive and experience with all your senses, without any mental distraction and with the elimination of commenting on what is happening on the part of your mind, you also experience.

4. ACCEPT/CHANGE/LEAVE

Do not fight against what has happened. Strengthen the acceptance.
(Kurt Haberstich (*1948), Swiss author and aphorist)

Nothing changes unless we change.
(Unknown)

If you want to play a leading role, you have to leave the scenes.
(Martin Gerhard Reisenberg (*1949), graduate librarian and author)

4.1 What does accepting/changing/leaving mean?

From a spiritual point of view, you can either a) accept situations or problems, b) change them, or c) leave them.

> ➢ **Accept means to accept the situation or problem one hundred percent, as it is.**
> ➢ **To change in this context means to actively (want to) change the situation.**
> ➢ **If accepting or changing a situation does not satisfy you, you can always leave it.**

These three options are always freely available to you. What is the best solution for you? The answer may vary depending on the situation.

4.2 How can I accept, change and leave?

You can better accept all situations in which you find yourself in life if you look back on the problems in which you have already found yourself and subsequently recognize and become aware of the positive and the lessons learned from them. This leads to a changed knowledge and consciousness in you, so that you can also learn from currently difficult situations and draw positive things from them.

Since you will henceforth live consciously and succeed in letting go of useless and obstructive things, you will experience high-quality inspiration to change situations. You will now also speak out what you may have suppressed at an earlier time.

If you cannot cope with accepting and changing in the respective situations or problems, you have the freedom to leave them at any time. You are a mature human being and determine as a sovereign over your life.

4.3 Why does accepting/changing/leaving strengthen my personality?

You develop a feeling for why something was good in the past, because you can draw a positive lesson from every past situation. Consequently, you will be able to decide more quickly whether to accept a new situation or problem, or to try to change it or leave it. Your actions will become clearer and more unambiguous.

A lengthy weighing of decisions to be made is outdated. Thereby you do not build up inner resistance and blockades anymore and you can let yourself fall into the respective task (which should always mean for you: accept - change - or let go).

Through this clear setting of your personal situation compass, you develop a greater trust in life and yourself. You will develop your own sensitivity and feel that life supports you. You learn to decide more intuitively.

4.4 How does accepting/changing/leaving contribute to my wealth?

You deal with so-called "problems" differently. A former and much respected colleague once told me that there are no problems at all only challenges. He was right in his assessment. Simply renaming a problem a challenge makes it seem much more manageable. In addition, you can grow from a challenge.

You will develop a clear inner compass ("nerves of steel") in order to be able, for example, to ride out bad phases and face them with this in mind. You say in your annual salary discussion exactly why you should receive more money (= change). You quit because you have tried long enough to change the situation in your personal work environment (= let go). You always have confidence in life and are sure that - to continue the above example - something better is coming or waiting for you.

Concretely and related to your wealth you can change e.g. the following: You finally start to shift your portfolio from single stocks to ETFs and funds, which you have wanted to do for a long time. Alternatively, you finally sell the poorly rented house inherited from your parents in order to invest the proceeds in high-yield investments. You finally invest the money that is lying around in call money accounts or savings books and is eaten up by the annual inflation.

Here are my ETF buy recommendations for those willing to change. I advise the following purchases: The USA-S&P 500 from Black Rock with the Security

Identification Number (WKN) or International Security Identification Number (ISIN): IE00B5BMR087. This is a passive accumulating fund, i.e. the profits are reinvested. The fund volume is very large with more than 50 billion euros. The costs are very favorable at 0.07% per year. The fund represents 97% of the largest companies in the USA.

The USA-S&P 500 is also available in a distributing version. The publisher Vanguard, for example, also issues a low-cost version with ISIN: IE00B3XXRP09 (0.07% p.a.).

4.5 What are the idioms about accepting/changing/leaving?

I have picked out three examples for each of these three topics:

Accept:

1.) Life happens. Your rejection or acceptance shows your attitude towards life (Irina Rauthmann).

2.) Life: Breathe in and breathe out. Accept and give away. Finding and losing (Torsten Marold)

3.) Death is a part of life. When we accept our own mortality, our own finitude, we can focus on what we really want in this earthly life (Dörthe Huth).

The first example of accepting points out or asks you if you are swimming along with the current of life or if you are building up resistance to life. In this context, swimming along is in no way to be viewed negatively. Basically, rejecting is a questionable way. As mentioned above, you should ... accept, change or leave.

The second example points out another very important aspect: giving away. Reflect on how much material and psychological garbage you carry around with you. Free yourself from it!

The last phrase is the most important from the selected examples. Accepting death - and thus overcoming the fear of death - is a central point in order to be able to accept yourself at all.

fear of death - is a central point in order to be able to accept yourself at all.

Change:

4.) The greatest decision of your life lies in the fact that you can change your life by changing your mindset (Albert Schweitzer).

5.) Others cannot change anything in my life (Justus Vogt).

6.) The reassuring thing about playing the lottery: I can pretend to want to change my life, but will never be embarrassed (Stefan Rogal).

All three examples about changing are very good from my point of view. Albert Schweitzer even glorifies the ability to change one's mindset as the greatest decision of life, which remains a life task until the end.

That only you can change something in your life is illustrated by the second saying.

Many people attach conditions to changes in their lives, such as winning the lottery. This kind of reasoning can often be observed among people who do not really want to change anything in their lives.

Leave:

7.) "To make the best of it" means only to submit with decency into a bad situation (Thomas S. Lutter)!

8.) Commanders must bring the led only into an out-glueless situation. The rest is done by the instinct of self-preservation (unknown author).

9.) Every situation is to be endured, to which we can react by acting (Johann Mutius).

Making a bad compromise and living with it is sometimes more difficult than consistently leaving a situation. Many of us grew up with the first proverb due to an upbringing by parents who grew up in the post-war years. However, it should no longer apply today, as we no longer live in times of need in our society.

What do you do in an apparently hopeless situation? You try to leave it! The selected example wants to point to it. How often do you accept a situation that you inwardly define as hopeless and thus endure it?

The last example also deals with bearing. Reacting in action is the same as abandoning. How often exactly do we not do that?

5. FEARLESSNESS

Do not be afraid of change, change fear.
(Bernd Sieberichs (*1961), local writer)

5.1 What does fearlessness mean?

Probably every human being has some form of fear. This is already laid into our cradle.

> **There is basically**
> **a) The concrete fear, if e.g. physical integrity threatens or**
> **b) The fear of indeterminacy.**
> **Fearlessness means to be free of both fears.**

From my point of view, the fear of indeterminacy (also uncertainty, insecurity) often arises in people who think and live in a past-oriented way. From the negative experiences of the past often arises grief and afterwards a certain disorientation as well as the doubting of his own self-image.

The fear regarding expected threats or uncertainties can rather be described as stress. As a rough formula, the following should be kept in mind: "Anxious" people tend to think in terms of the past, "Stressed" people tend to think in terms of the future. However, both types are afraid of the uncertain.

5.2 How can I be fearless?

The past-oriented thinker ("scaredy-cat") can counter the burgeoning fear with gratitude. Gratitude for everything he was allowed to experience in life so far, what he has achieved which people he was allowed to get to know. Gratitude exercises can and should be practiced every day, for example by summing up in the evening for which event you are grateful today.

The future-oriented thinker ("stressed") can define a clearer goal for his further life, which should be as concrete as possible. The past-oriented thinker can become aware that possibly no goal setting is necessary at all. This seems like a contradiction at first, but it depends on the type. In the next chapter, this aspect will be discussed in more detail.

If one follows my thought and recognizes that most people think either past-oriented or future-oriented, the question why we are so little present and thus live in the now, answers itself almost by itself. However, if you want to live without fear, you should spend a large part of your life in the here and now.

5.3 Why does fearlessness strengthen my personality?

Through gratitude exercises (for past-oriented people), which by the way should also be carried out by the stressed (future-oriented people), you will notice with time that - besides the issues for which you are grateful - you have definitely experienced moments of success (as you define success for yourself). This will take away your insecurity bit by bit.

A concrete goal can lead to the fact that you spend less time with trivialities and focus more on your goals (if you want to define some for yourself). You become more effective and creative in your thinking; the space for fearful thoughts becomes smaller. In your personality, a direction becomes recognizable, because you treat, for example, trivialities as such.

A stronger presence in the present will bring you greater attention from those around you. You can achieve this by reducing both your past and future thinking, e.g. by talking to your fellow men and being absorbed in the here and now. In this way, you will be listened to better, because you will also listen more concentrated.

5.4 How does fearlessness contribute to my wealth?

In business meetings and private conversations, you achieve full focus, attention and concentration of your counterpart, because your thoughts are not lost in another time plane.

Your conversation partners honor your complete presence. Fear cannot be detected in your behavior, which makes all your conversations of higher quality and therefore more successful.

You make courageous decisions without fear, because you know that their consequences will not kill you and that you have made them as a sovereign. Therefore, you can be sure to be able to estimate the consequences well.

A little more concretely related to your wealth, fearlessness means staying invested. It really does not do you any good to have large amounts of cash reserves in savings accounts, call money accounts or even at home. You should be able to access a maximum of 10% of your assets relatively quickly. These may well be call money accounts. With the majority however, thus then 90% should be invested like e.g. in financial investments (ETF's, funds, shares) or real estates.

Here my ETF purchase recommendations for fearless. I advise you to buy the following: The MSCI World Information Technology from Lyxor with the Security Identification Number (WKN) or International Security Identification Number (ISIN): LU0533033667. This is a passive accumulating fund, i.e. the profits are reinvested. The fund volume is large with more than 1 billion euros. The costs are favorable at 0.30% per year. The fund tracks the largest IT companies in the world.

5.5 What are the idioms about fearlessness?

The idioms on the subject of fear are often about how to face it or how to overcome it. I have put together four here:

1.) Who is no longer afraid of fear, can live fearlessly (Matthias Weser).

2.) When the fear of death is overcome, the joy of life can begin (Günter J. Ammon).

3.) A person can only be the person he wants to be when he has freed himself from his fear of speaking and leading (Jennifer Victoria Withelm).

4.) Love destroys all evil and makes free from all fear (Hildegard von Bingen).

I have included the truism of the first example as an example because simplicity is often the key. Imagine a fearless life in which there are few limits for you.

The second example points out once again the great importance of the fear of death. If you accept your finiteness, you can develop more joy.

The third example comes more from the direction of management/ leadership seminars. When you can speak and lead fearlessly in front of and with others, then you can be who you want to be.

Love - and here from my point of view especially self-love, as described in the second chapter - should help you to free yourself from fears.

6. GOAL SETTING

Do not pursue other people's goals, and you will always reach your
goal.
(Andreas Tenzer (*1954), German philosopher and educator)

6.1 What does it mean to set a goal?

Are you drifting aimlessly or are you pursuing specific life goals? Where are you currently in your goal pursuit?

> ➢ **Goals are statements about desired states in the future that are to be achieved through appropriate ("goal-oriented") human behavior.**
> **You can think about setting goals, but you do not have to.**

Goal setting can cause stress, especially for the more future-oriented person. However, do you need (personal) goal setting at all?

You may already be exposed to annual goal setting in your company, which is derived from corporate goal setting (e.g. sales targets, profit targets, cost targets, etc.). Now you should consider setting additional personal goals in your life and how you will live/create the achievement of those goals.

From my point of view, the question of goal setting also depends on your personal character or profile. There are people who need a short- and long-term goal (e.g. a best possible graduation, becoming rich, etc.) and others who can live completely without a goal (e.g. existence for the period of a life is a gift for me, I will design it optimally for me).

There are dangers in both ways of life: Setting goals too high may frustrate you if you do not achieve them; setting goals too low may make you arrogant. Living without goals can significantly reduce well-being for people who actually need a compass because they lack direction. People who live without goal setting can despair of surrendering to the daily here and now.
What type are you?

6.2 How do I find out if I need a goal?

How do you determine if you need (personal) goals? First of all, you need to be clear about whether your thinking is more past or future oriented.

As described in the previous chapter, the future-oriented thinker (the more stressed type) can define a clearer goal for his future life (as concrete or evaluated as possible). With long-term goals (approx. over ten years), the objective can be quite ambitious. Due to the gained life experience, an adjustment (upwards or downwards) will take place over the years anyway. However, the short-term target (about one year) should be achievable in any case in order not to discourage oneself. The period for goal setting can also be much shorter; for example, if you are preparing for an athletic competition or for an exam.

The past-oriented thinker can realize that goal setting may not be necessary at all. He should consciously observe his here and now situations and becomes more and more confident in his own positioning in the current scenery.

To be clear: If you are more future-oriented, then set goals. If you are past-oriented, then you can possibly do without them.

6.3 Why does a positioning for goal setting strengthen my personality?

Through clear positioning, which either includes goal setting or does without it, you strengthen your inner compass. You know what you need, what is good for you and how you want to live.

It is crucial that you find out for yourself whether you need a goal setting or not.

6.4 How does goal-setting positioning contribute to my wealth?

Goals may or may not be material. In the books of wealthy financial gurus, one can often read that they have become rich mainly because of other motivations. From my point of view, there is reason to doubt this, since some things are glorified and glorified in retrospect. I think it is all about how you approach and pursue your goals (whether material or ideal). Beside the what and how of the goal control, which is particularly important for goal-oriented humans, is important for humans, who do not pursue a goal, as who one goes through the life.

Negative occupied behaviors such as ruthlessness and selfishness may get you to material goals faster; however, your personality will be steered in a direction you may never have wanted to go.

A strengthened portion of self-confidence and an alert listening into your own being-self can arise with both directions, a clearly defined goal pursuit and a consciously lived aimless approach. Only, it should be clear to you when you want to live which approach. You can also switch between both approaches: In some areas of life live goal-oriented and in others rather let things come to you.

In terms of material wealth and investment behavior, I think there are two general directions you can go: You invest radically in future themes, such as blockchain technology, cryptocurrencies, IT companies and the like with a correspondingly high risk, or you go more into

ETF's or funds that have a much broader risk spread. Even with the latter, you can put accents in different industries or technologies. Maybe a mixture of the two directions makes sense.

Here are my ETF purchase recommendations for ambitious target setters. I advise you to buy the following: the CoinShare Global Blockchain from Invesco with the security identification number (WKN) or International Security Identification Number (ISIN): IE00BGBN6P67. This is a passive accumulating fund, meaning that profits are reinvested. The fund size is large with more than 1 billion euros. Costs are within reason at 0.65% per year. The fund provides access to global companies from developed and emerging markets that participate in the blockchain ecosystem.

6.5 What are the idioms about goal setting?

There are many idioms and even more articles on the topic of goal setting, especially in management literature. I have selected three examples here:

1.) Setting a goal is easy. Ignoring it is even easier (Willy Meurer).

2.) I do not set a goal for my God, He gives me little or much; Blessed is he who is content; He lives content at his best' (unknown author)!

3.) Set your goals big enough and the circumstances will follow (unknown author).

Whether you are the type who needs a goal or not, as described above, you should find out yourself. If you are clear about it, you will not get into the dilemma described in the idiom of setting a goal and then ignoring it. From my point of view, it is not so easy to ignore a goal you set yourself. For example, if you set yourself the goal of losing three kilograms and then back off from it (for whatever reason), you may cause yourself great frustration if you cannot get the goal you once set out of your mind.

The poem of the second example refers in the core generally to objectives. From my point of view, the author wants to express that one lives a content-rich life if one accepts everything as God grants it to one.

The content of the third example is also often used in motivational literature. Especially in the case of long-term goals (for example, over a period of 10 years), the goal cannot be high enough. The circumstances change because you change...

7. COPY PATTERNS

Many find their own way
by copying.
(Andrea Mira Meneghin (*1967))

7.1 What does it mean to copy patterns?

Did you used to copy from the person sitting next to you in a written exam at school? You used to copy from your neighbor when you knew that he had learned more, was much better at the subject, or you did not know what to do. Why are you too proud today to use successful models, perhaps somewhat modified, for yourself? Do you think you are educated enough today that you do not need to and that the brilliant idea of your life will come to you? Life is too short to relive the (negative) experiences of others.

> ➤ **Copying patterns is copying or imitating trend-setting or successful examples (people, things, business models).**

There is nothing harmful about copying successful life models, behaviors or concepts of other people, as long as you do not copy products or ideas, which can get you into legal trouble.

7.2 How can I successfully copy patterns?

Take a look at the blueprints of others. They are available for little money in thousands of biographies of successful people. Just pick out the people who are very close to your definition of success. This does not necessarily have to be related to monetary wealth. Success can be defined in many different ways.

Are there people in the world (politicians, entrepreneurs, inventors, etc.) who inspire you? Why do these people fascinate you? Try to find out. Maybe your parents are still positive role models for you today. Why is that so? Which behavior do you remember particularly well? Get clarity about it!

If you like the behavior or thought patterns of one of your idols, why you do not simply imitate them? This is not stealing ideas; otherwise, the person would not reveal it. Everyone is free to learn from mistakes as well as from positively valued patterns. Perhaps your ego prevents you from doing so, because the approach does not originate from you. You should throw these doubts overboard, because the gain in time for you will be enormous. People always learn from each other, because man is a social being.

7.3 Why does pattern matching strengthen my personality?

The exact knowledge, which good and/or positive behaviors one takes over (or has taken over), can lead to excellent modifications of these. What has already been proven is thereby improved over time and possibly even adapted to the spirit of the times.

Your personality is strengthened, because you can be sure that you do good things even better and work practically only with success models. You are aware of the fact that you will have much more positive than negative experience.

It is similar when you play in a good soccer team and here I can speak from my personal experience: If you move to a higher class/league, where the individual players are usually more talented, and play there, you will automatically get better as well. Why is that? Because in the many training sessions with your teammates, you pick up the good behaviors in the game and integrate them into your own routines. This is a prime example of successfully learning patterns.

7.4 How does pattern matching add to my wealth?

Sometimes a good idea is simply missing the last building block. Why should this not come from you? Bill Gates did not develop the operating system DOS himself. However, he had an idea of how to market it and how it might be accepted.

The above example is a very well known one. If you take over e.g. only the positive things from the fund of your parents and/or from your own education into the education of your children, then that is already a substantial positive advancement.

Furthermore, you can save a lot of time if you do not repeat mistakes that others have already made. It is a necessity to learn from your own mistakes, but it is an art to learn from the mistakes of others.

What does this mean specifically for your material wealth? This is actually relatively simple: Just look at successful investment models. Here are two examples. Elon Musk, currently the richest person in the world, has invested all the money he earned in his next project and is very successful with it. But how high is the probability that such an approach works and is successful? I claim, in 99.9% of the cases it does not work and this approach has features of a va-banque player. I hope this kind of investing does not serve as an example for you. I would rather keep it with people like Warren Buffet. The American investor (certainly still in the top 10 richest people in the world) has developed a solid investment strategy over the years and examines potential investment companies very carefully before investing.

In addition to these very prominent but also very opposite investors, there are many other personalities that may be a better fit for you if you are looking for an investor role model.

Here is my ETF buying recommendation for skimmers. Here is what I advise you to buy: the iShares NASDAQ-100 from Black Rock with the security identification number (WKN) or International Security Identification Number (ISIN): DE000A0F5UF5. This is a passive distributing fund, i.e. the profits are distributed regularly. The fund volume is large with more than 3 billion euros. The costs are within the limits with 0.31% per year. The fund tracks the NASDAQ-100.

7.5 What idioms are there on the subject of pattern checking?

From whom can one still copy something today? From nature and from successful models. This approach can lay a good foundation for your own further development. Here are three sayings:

1.)   Nature makes the patterns - man only copies those (Klaus Klages).

2.)   Just as one does not always have to imitate, so one does not have to want to be peculiar right from the start; one continues to train on a pattern until one develops morally oneself and takes shape (Ernst von Feuchtersleben).

3.)   A great pattern arouses emulation and gives higher laws to judgment (Friedrich von Schiller).

The first saying states that man has always copied nature and - from my point of view - has done well with it. One thinks for example of the realizations with the subject of flying and the derivations of birds.

The second example explains well in the second part what I would like to express in the whole chapter: Educate yourself on a pattern until you can develop it further, modify it or adopt it yourself.

Friedrich von Schiller points out that "great" patterns naturally inspire emulation. You should also do this without having a bad conscience.

8. FEEL SECURITY

Those who seek absolute security find despair.
(Unknown)

8.1 What does feeling security mean?

No risk - no fun? Can you achieve the security in your life that is sufficient for a comfortable life? Here, unfortunately, I have to disappoint you right at the beginning of this chapter. The security you are looking for (possibly) does not exist.

> **Security is a state of being outwardly non-threatened (e.g. dangers to life and limb) as well as the absence of perceived dangers (e.g. poverty, hunger, education).**

Why do so many people look for security in their lives? From my point of view, this is on the one hand genetically conditioned, on the other hand also historically explicable. For example, some women look for men who can "provide" enough (material) for their children. Furthermore, wars and their hard post-war years have caused people to want to create so-called "cushions".

Are you aware, however, that you could be dead

tomorrow (e.g. due to a traffic accident or an infarction)? What advantages do you then ultimately have in terms of security?

8.2 How do I feel security?

This may seem a bit weird to you now: but it should be clear to you that there is no such thing as security. It is an individual feeling. You can be hit by a stroke of fate from one day to the next, for which you cannot insure yourself in advance.

With this certainty and the fact that you live in a welfare state that will not let you starve, the question remains: What is supposed to happen to you? You can arm yourself against illnesses in part by, for example, living healthily or thinking positively, which has a lasting effect on your psyche and is thus beneficial for your body.

Against the external threat, there are doors and also locks. On some family houses, you can even see bars in front of the windows on the first floor. As we have already said, security is above all a personal feeling. However, the feeling about it can also become a prison...

Oh yes, one more thing: You certainly will not learn to feel safe if you regularly watch TV shows dealing with true crimes. If you look at the number of detective stories on TV, which are mainly about murder and manslaughter, you almost have to assume that people's sense of insecurity wants to be nourished.

8.3 Why does a clear positioning on the subject of feeling safe strengthen my personality?

If it is clear to you that security does not actually exist

or is only a feeling, you can and will live more courageously. You will probably finally make the decisions that you have been putting off for a long time.

You will also no longer radiate fearfulness, since there is virtually nothing to be afraid of. Furthermore, you will become more predictable for yourself and others, since you will not shirk from making decisions.

What should actually prevent you from believing yourself to be in constant security?

Your newly gained clarity in decisions creates a clear inner structure and stabilizes your self-confidence. This is because you no longer have to weigh up for so long whether the respective decision is good or bad. This long weighing can possibly drive you to an inner confusion. A decision is a decision; whether it is good or bad usually turns out much later. In addition, most of the time, a decision made quickly reflects what you actually think or want.

8.4 How does positioning myself on my sense of security contribute to my wealth?

After you have clearly positioned yourself with regard to your personal sense of security, you can - as already mentioned above - make decisions that you have been putting off for a long time, such as whether you want to buy an apartment or a house or whether you prefer to invest your money in shares, funds or ETFs. You are also no longer afraid of so-called pension gaps, which the insurance industry is constantly trying to convince you of. Therefore, you do not take any nonsensical insurances and are therefore not over insured.

You finally take that trip around the world you have wanted to take for so long. You have enough self-confidence that you can continue working in your profession and you know that the experiences you will make will enrich you.

By making conscious and sovereign decisions, you are not stuck in a hamster wheel that may block you, but actively determine your own life. Thereby you have the possibility to change to the fast lane.

For your material wealth, this can mean that you are now ready to try out other forms of investment than overnight money accounts or real estate. You are looking into funds and ETF's and testing some out, too.

Here is my ETF purchase recommendation for security investors. I advise you to buy the MSCI World Quality from DWS with the Security Identification Number

(WKN) or International Security Identification Number (ISIN): IE00BL25JL35. This is a passive accumulating fund, i.e. the profits are reinvested. The fund size is large with more than 1 billion euros. Costs are low at 0.25% per year. The fund tracks companies from the MSCI World that have a top balance sheet.

8.5 What idioms are there on the subject of feeling safe?

I have found two very appropriate expressions for this.

1.) Since I have understood that there can be no security in life and in love, I am no longer afraid of losing it (Ernst Ferstl).

2.) Always being on the go, that is what I call life. To be lulled by security means certain death (Oscar Wilde).

The first idiom establishes a great connection between security and fear. Namely, the fear of loss. This kind of fear is always based on the actual primal fear of death. If you, too, have correctly understood that your life is finite, you can also find a different and new positioning on the subject of "feeling fear".

Oscar Wilde expresses in the above quoted saying the boredom that can arise when you are lulled by too much security. For him, it is even fatal. There is a very good book by Osho on this subject, from my point of view. The book "Courage" has the subtitle "Live wild and dangerous". In it, this topic is dealt with excellently. For him, the willingness to live in uncertainty is courage. The willingness to be unsecured is for him trust (in life itself). Furthermore, awareness is for him the only right way to face uncertainty.

An important saying of Osho in this context is: "Don't talk about uncertainty, call it freedom".

9 SUMMARIES OF THE EIGHT DEFINITIONS

For better clarity and memorization, I have summarized all the important definitions again here. For me, the themes described in the eight chapters above, in combination, are the keys to personal wealth - letting go, self-love, consciousness, accepting/changing/ leaving, fearlessness, goal setting, copying patterns, and security:

> Letting go is the ability to not be attached to something/someone.

> Self-love is the comprehensive acceptance of oneself through unrestricted love for oneself.

> Consciousness is the actual experience of mental states of conscience.

> Acceptance means to accept the situation or problem one hundred percent, as it is.

To change means to actively change (want to change) a situation.

If accepting or changing a situation does not satisfy you, you can always leave it.

> Fear
There is basically:

a) The concrete fear, e.g. when one is threatened with bodily harm or
b) The fear of indeterminacy.

Fearlessness means to be free from both fear states (concrete fear, fear of indeterminacy).

➤ Goals are statements about desired states in the future, which are to be reached by appropriate ("goal-oriented") human behavior.

You can have goals, but you do not have to.

➤ Copying patterns is the copying or imitation of trend-setting or successful examples (people, things, business models).

➤ Security is a state of not being threatened externally (e.g. dangers to life and limb) and the absence of perceived dangers (e.g. poverty, hunger, education).

10 BRIEFLY EXPLAINED: HOW CAN I IMPLEMENT EFFECTIVELY?

To give you a quick guide on how you can most effectively address the eight building blocks I've addressed and initiate change, I've listed the relevant keys here again in a striking way:

➢ Let go
Trust yourself

➢ Self-love
Treat yourself like someone you really love.

➢ Live consciousness
Observe the now without judgment

➢ Accept - Change - Leave
Decide for yourself situationally for one of the alternatives

➢ Fearlessness
Live the biggest part of your life in the here and now

➢ Goal setting
Position yourself if you need goal setting

➢ Check out patterns
Continue to develop what is good/proven

➢ Feel security
Live with the certainty that does not exist.

Anything that is attached to you is what holds you back the most from letting go. Many attachments come from your childhood and your parents' upbringing. You can start trusting yourself now.

If you actively promote your personal development, you will also learn again to strengthen your love for yourself and to accept yourself. Self-development motivates. Above all, work on your behavior.

Through non-judgmental observation of situations in which you find yourself, you will most quickly achieve a changed consciousness and possibly draw completely different conclusions through non-judgment.

Situational decision-making in the three options of accept - change - leave will probably be interpreted as an emotional reaction at first (especially when you leave a situation), but in time you will become certain in your decision whether you can accept or change a situation or whether you have to leave it. In addition, it does not matter how others interpret your reaction.

You will best succeed in freeing yourself from fear by reviewing your position on dying and death. Clarity about the finitude of your own life can give you wings.

Whether or not there is a goal, you should be at peace with yourself about whether or not there should be one for you. If you have one, pursue it consistently; if you do not have one, live accordingly.

If you continue to develop the tried and tested or simply copy patterns, you will see that you will soon be able to develop your own creations from them.

If you have recognized that security, as you possibly define it for yourself, does not exist, you will experience an inner liberation, which will let you live relaxed and detached.

11. SUCCESS FORMULAS TO ACHIEVE EVERYTHING

If you want to make the most of yourself and your life, you should be aware of the following points during a self-analysis:

- Become aware of your attachments

- Accept yourself, because you are the star in your life

- Live in the now, especially through persistent observation.

- Recognize the positive in your life and learn from it.

- Be grateful for what you have experienced so far

- Get clear about what makes you tick (past-oriented / future-oriented)

- Be clear about role models

- Security, no matter how you define it, does not exist.

Can you remember praise and recognition from your

childhood or school days? Why do we find this so difficult? In addition, why do we tend to remember reprimands or condemnations, even though children voiced some of these? Write down which positive remarks you experienced in your childhood (from parents, teachers and friends). You will see that these are still valid today and you can become aware of your strengths again and strengthen them further (i.e.: strengthen your strengths). Moreover, make clear to yourself why negative statements (about you) stick to you or remain stuck.

In the book "The Fifth Promise" by Don Miguel Ruiz, it is described very well that, for example, in a family everyone looks at the same situations from a completely different perspective and thus develops his own truth about it. That is also completely understandable, since everyone has his subjective perception. This is also true for you. The topic is explained very clearly in the book with the help of different movie theaters in which the same film is shown, but is viewed by different viewers and therefore interpreted differently. Become the clear: The star in your movie (life) is you. In addition, as a star you can allow yourself your airs.

Do you want to decelerate your life and thus generate more lived time? Then you should arrive in the here and now as quickly as possible. How can you do that? Through persistent observation and participation (presence) in situations in which you find yourself. Do not be stuck in the past and especially do not rehash yesterday's problems and victim roles. On the other hand, do not continuously paint your future with bright colors. First, make sure that you perform in the present by being fully present and participating.

I have already written about the positive moments in your life in the first commentary.

As I have already described in the thematic chapters, gratitude is an important feeling to counter anxiety. However, this feeling is equally important for self-reflection, to highlight and be clear about the positive circumstances in your life.

If you know whether you are more of a past- or future-oriented person, then you can realign yourself more effectively.

I have already commented on the subject of role models above: Reading autobiographies can help you successfully adopt thought patterns. Moreover, that with certainty...

12. SUCCESS FORMULAS FOR PERSONALITY DEVELOPMENT

Important messages for your personal development:

> Letting go is an important prerequisite for achieving personal freedom.

> Self-love strengthens your self-confidence, self-awareness, and obvious virtues.

> Living in full consciousness leads to presentness.

> The classification Accept - Change - Leave leads to unambiguous action.

> Fearlessness leads to a more effective and creative way of thinking.

> Positioning for goal setting strengthens your inner compass.

> Pattern checking ensures working with success models and saves time.

> Positioning for safety promotes courageous decisions.

The self-confident attainment of personal freedom takes place through self-love, present-mindedness and unambiguous action. Fearlessness and an inner compass allows success models to emerge via courageous decisions.

The preceding small paragraph is a core statement of this book. If you are aware of these two sentences, then you have already taken many of the thinking approaches described by me.

The success formulas described above are called into question from a wide variety of directions. I will deal with some of them in the following.

Personal freedom and ultimately happiness are topics that many strive for and to which every person is basically entitled. Unfortunately, our mind keeps us from permanently experiencing and feeling these feelings. After all, he (the mind) is constantly speaking to us and is at the same time our sharpest judge. In principle, the mind wants to tell us that freedom and happiness must first be earned. However, this demand of our mind has no justification. The claim to freedom and happiness you acquire with your birth.

The mind meets letting go with doubt. It makes you doubt whether you can really trust your own decision-making. That means in principle, the mind questions yourself! Moreover, we allow this thinking for years! How can self-love and self-confidence develop at all? In newer spiritual books, it is described that the self does not consist of the mind and not of the body. They are only tools to be used when needed.

Self-love is mostly put into doubt by statements that

others make about you and that you believe (at least in part). This means you carry beliefs about yourself whose origins you should question. If these negative beliefs come up in you, you should first allow them, welcome them, and not disqualify them. The more often you look at them, you will experience that they are completely unfounded in substance.

The past and the future keep us from living in full consciousness. Through our constant mental "chewing over" or setting up "what if - scenarios", we forget to be present in the now.

You can use your mind, for example, in the classification of situation in "Accept - Change - Leave". Nevertheless, what do we do? We react emotionally and usually aggravate the situation. Even worse: We burden ourselves with it. Therefore, it would be advisable here to leave these emotions outside.

The path to fearlessness is torpedoed by many influences. Your company may make you afraid of a possible job loss, insurance companies because of a discovered pension gap and inflation makes you think about old age poverty. Here it is worth to look deep inside and to question the truth or the probability; otherwise, a creative way of thinking can hardly develop.

Your clear inner compass is shaken by often changing objectives. Since the world and our environment are spinning much faster than before digitalization due to technology, more goal adjustments may be necessary than before. Here, it makes sense to think about fewer objectives.

If your model for success is based in part on "pattern copying," there may be a headwind about the immediate society around you that frowns upon "copying." However, this should leave you unaffected, as the most important models of success have been created in this way. Originality is nice but life is simply too short for it and often it only comes about through luck and coincidence anyway.

Close people who fear disadvantages for themselves (from your decisions) often doubt your courageous decisions, which can be quite small at the beginning.

13. SUCCESS FORMULAS OF YOUR WEALTH

To support the above main theses, I have again compiled a short list of supporting mindsets and commotions:

Mindset:

- Focus yourself by letting go of secondary issues.

- Be selfish in a positive way: "What do I get out of this?"

- Be fully present and present

- Look at problems as challenges

- In goal setting, the "how" is essential

- Don't take on victim or martyr roles

To-do's:

- Listen carefully!

- Be focused, attentive and concentrated!

- Rearrange your priorities!

- Big deals have a big impact; small deals have a small impact!

- Make bold decisions without fear!

- Be clear in your objectives!

- Develop the proven in a positive way!

- Copy and modify success models, develop mutations!

- Develop your personal strategy as well as your success formula and success calculation!

- Adjust your personal compass new and clear!

The preceding ways of thinking and to-do's are explained in the following also based on concrete examples more exactly.

13.1 Secondary issues

What is meant by letting go of secondary issues? Here is an example: Question how much time you spend watching TV on a daily or weekly basis. What TV shows do you watch? I know this from my own experience: the leisurely evening after a day's work tempts you to watch the media. However, what do you personally get out of it when the Democrats fight with the Republicans again in the U.S. or the former American president tweets something unbelievable? You can be outraged about it, but what does it do for you personally? Even the third rerun of a movie you love, which happens to start just after the daytime news, robs you of your precious time if you do not hit the off button on the remote. That, too, can be letting go. In this context, secondary means to me wasting time on topics that do not contribute to your personal development (and thus to your wealth). Of course, you should also create oases of peace for yourself, where you can relax and rest. Nevertheless, choose them consciously and do not let yourself be tempted to watch TV. When you watch television, do it selectively (e.g., when you watch specific documentaries). Why don't you replace television with reading books that interest you thematically? I know that sounds like a mother talking to her twelve-year-old son who is lazy about reading. However, through the selection process alone that you experience (Which topics really interest me?), you might find out many new things about yourself.

My modules, Your wealth

13.2 What is my benefit?

In the western world, we live in a kind of social market economy. We are already taught in our upbringing that taxes are important for a redistribution in our society. The acceptance for a redistribution can be seen especially in the fact that the tax honesty in the western world is very high compared to other regions. You, too, make your contribution to the common good by paying your taxes every month. In private life, however, there must be limits to your participation in the common good. Why? Because often the basic willingness to get involved is exploited by other people. After all, in my view, people who have a high level of social commitment are easily recognized by their social actions. Social behavior and commitment should come from within and the decision where and whether to get involved should be made freely and independently. Unfortunately, I have personally experienced it many times that the socially engaged people are exploited by others, in which they are additionally driven into more and more new engagements, just because they may not be able to say no. This leads to a total overload of the already committed and at the end of their working life; they wonder why their own pension is so low. I definitely do not want to discourage you from getting involved socially, because I think it is an important aspect for our society and your personal development. However, always question, if you are asked to do so by others, how much you are already doing and what a further burden would mean for you personally.

13.3 Presence

I have been working on my personal presence all my life. I am physically present in the appropriate situations, which is clear. However, the question is, in what way do I want to be present? In addition, what keeps me from being present in the way I want to be present (e.g., paying full attention to the others present)? It is the judgments, biases, and future/past oriented thoughts that keep me from being more personally present. This is exactly what I keep catching myself doing. I think it is my personal task to learn to engage with situations in a non-judgmental way, thereby allowing myself to have a presence as I envision it. For example, I unconsciously evaluate the conversation situation I get into, the interlocutors involved, who may already be pigeonholed in my mind, as well as past conversation situations from which little may have come out. All these thoughts keep me from giving more presence. You would have to hit some kind of reset button before each new conversation to erase the biases and, in some cases, pre-judgments. Let us work together to make our presence better.

13.4 Challenges

Why do I think it is important to view problems as challenges? Even the word problem in itself has a negative connotation in society. Comparably, you could literally "put obstacles in your own way" or "put sticks between your legs"; all of these expressions represent obstacles. When you solve problems (or remove obstacles) in your life, you may check them off after they are done. When you classify a problem as a challenge, however, you make it clear from the beginning that you feel personally challenged to work out a solution that you can possibly grow with and that will last for a longer period. By consciously working out a solution, your personality grows as your wealth of experience in finding a solution becomes broader. On the way to finding a solution, there may also be setbacks. Here, from my point of view, it is important how you formulate these "setbacks" for yourself. The wording for a setback can also be experience, for example. A positive wording can give wings to the personality development.

13.5 Goal setting: What and how and as who?

In a company for which I worked for a long time, one day they came up with the idea to fundamentally revise and at the same time simplify the annual target system, which was agreed upon individually with each employee. From my point of view, they had the ingenious suggestion to assess and evaluate not only the content-related goals (question: "What should be achieved"?) but also the way of implementation at the end of the year (question: "How should something be achieved"?). Both focal points were weighted at 50% each. Thus, attention was paid not only to the content of the objective, but also to the way in which an objective is approached and achieved. The effects on the leadership culture and on the implementation of the content objectives in the company were enormously positive. In some cases, the content objectives were significantly exceeded, because colleagues were involved, timely agreements were made, and the objectives were discussed more frequently with managers. What do we learn from this? In goal setting, the "how" is essential! In newer spiritual guides, there is often an additional aspect, besides the one already mentioned above, regarding goal setting: "Who do you want to approach your goals as"? If you already approach, your goals in the role you are striving for, you will possibly come to other solutions than the ones you would find in your previous role when overcoming challenges.

13.6. Victim role

Taking on the role of a victim or martyr hinders you in the implementation of the success formula "Wealth". Why is that? First, you should recognize if you are in a victim role. I claim that many people do not even realize when they are in such a role. Alternatively, even worse: people consciously put themselves in a victim role so that they are shown sympathy and attention. In doing so, however, they demonstrate their powerlessness in the face of a system, a government, a boss, and so on. It is therefore important that you first recognize when or if you have fallen into a victim role and realize that by doing so you are basically giving away part of your personal power (the power of self-determination). The "fault" for your situation is usually not external circumstances, but you yourself, since your perception determines how you classify a situation. Consequently, someone who gives up some of their power by accepting a victim role, to others or to circumstances, should not be surprised if they no longer hold all the strings in their life.

However, if you are not a victim, then you may be a perpetrator. Perpetrators usually act; that is the crucial thing. They influence the course of their lives largely by consciously making their own decisions. By the way, I personally prefer the word doer instead of perpetrator, it does not sound so criminalizing.

13.7 Listen well

What is good listening and why is it so important? To put it briefly: Most people cannot. They lend you their ear, as they say colloquially, but the information goes (again colloquially) in on the left and out on the right. Good listening is active listening. However, what does that mean? As a listener, you are initially in a rather passive role, but you listen attentively to the content of what is being said and then ask intermediate and follow-up questions if you have not understood something correctly or fully. The conversation, in which you are predominantly passive as a listener, takes on a much higher quality through the queries and you really absorb the content of what is being said. In the process of listening, many people unfortunately let their ego get in the way - they are eager to tell their own stories and experiences. The consequence is that they focus on their own content, which they will immediately tell, and no longer really follow what the other person is saying.
I spent some time traveling the world as an auditor. That was easy money. Why? If you can listen well, people will tell you about their challenges in the work process. Investigative questioning is no longer necessary. You should definitely use the extraordinary lever of good listening for your personal development.

13.8 Focus

Focusing on the issues that are important to you is especially important when building wealth. Why is that? Because many people cannot define, which topics are important for them? Many always exclude and know very well what we do not want. In addition, through the constant exclusion they believe that the remaining quantity is so small at some point that it must be what one wants after all. However, this residual quantity will unfortunately never be so small that one can recognize a clear focus. Nevertheless, who knows exactly what he wants? Here an attentive self-observation is worthwhile. Last week I heard on the radio that the average person in industrialized countries owns 150,000 things. If you were asked what the ten to twenty most important things are for you, you would not really get there by a process of elimination. Even if you clean out regularly, you will not come up with these ten to twenty most important things. You have to actively position yourself. The classic question is: What three things would you take with you to a desert island? It is the same with focusing your topics. You have to actively define what is important to you. This can then lead to a personal investment strategy in financial topics.

13.9 Priorities

Reordering priorities is a constant companion on the path to wealth and can be seen as a logical consequence of focusing. Once you have defined the ten to twenty most important issues for you, you should also put them in an order.

However, priorities can also shift. What was important and correct yesterday may no longer apply today. Here is a concrete example: If you look at the topic of "investment", you could still earn good interest contributions with fixed-interest forms of investment or savings books twenty years ago. Today, if you do not switch to other forms of investment (for example, exchange-traded funds or actively managed funds), you lose money due to inflation and low interest rates. So even a re-prioritization is mandatory here if you do not want to lose money.

13.10. Big Deals

I have already talked in detail about the difference between small and large deals in the thematic chapters. Just maybe one more note on this: If you want to buy a house, think carefully whether this deal fits your personal wealth formula or not. Buying a house at the wrong time can more or less enslave you because you may be working for the house for the next thirty to forty years to pay off your debt. The state of the real estate market in recent years makes it virtually impossible for young families to purchase a home, despite low interest rates. Perhaps in this situation it is more prudent to invest first and wait for the market situation to calm down.

13.11. Courageous decisions

Which of your decisions do you consider outstandingly courageous in your life? For my life, I can answer this relatively easily: It is simply the seizing of opportunities that present themselves in the personal flow of life without too long a thought process.

Here are two examples with different implications: 1.) my employer offered me the opportunity to work abroad for a few years. The decision to do so, despite having small children in my luggage, was a courageous one for me personally, since it had to be made for and with an entire family, and my personal future was uncertain for the time thereafter. In retrospect, the decision to work abroad was an enrichment for all involved. 2.) SAP stock had a twenty percent drop in one day in 2021. Therefore, I bought in generously. This subsequent buying was also a courageous decision for me, but in retrospect certainly a good one. For me, a decision is courageous if the consequences are still uncertain. The consequences, however, and this is the most important thing, you can possibly influence positively or simply wait for the positive end. Therefore, in the first example, I was able to help teach my children, my wife, and myself about the culture of another country, thus positively influencing the consequences of the decision. In the second example, I simply waited for the positive recovery of the stock price.

13.12. Goal clarity

The more clear/concrete you are in your goal setting, the better you can shape the framework of your goal. Here is a comparison from everyday life: When you order a product on the Internet, you have to define very precisely, what you want to have: for example size, color, delivery mode, payment method, etc. Why don't you specify your personal objectives in a comparable way? You can align the general conditions to this concrete objective accordingly and possibly have other positive side aspects. Here are two examples: 1.) You want to save a certain amount of money per month, but you smoke two packs of cigarettes a day, which keeps you from reaching the desired savings amount. Here you can consider whether it would not make more sense to stop smoking to support your defined goal. 2.) You want to start your own business or possibly start your own company, but you hang out in front of the TV for four hours every night. At this point, you should rethink your priorities; otherwise, the company will not work out.

13.13. Further development and copying

Further development of what has been tried and tested is another important building block for your wealth. You do not have to make the mistakes that others have already made in developing themes or products. Just as you do not - literally - reinvent the wheel. There is nothing wrong with developing successful models (I have already explained this in the chapters above).

13.14. Strategy

In case you are pursuing a goal, you should develop a suitable strategy for it. A strategy should primarily define how the goal could best be achieved. For example, for a savings goal, define the savings opportunities; for an investment goal, define the risks to be taken. For both examples, you can clearly derive your success formula and income statement.

13.15. Compass

The best way to readjust your personal compass is to devote yourself primarily to the issues you have identified and prioritized. Whether or not there is a personal objective, do the things that are important to you either with full passion or not at all.

14 COMBINING SUCCESS FORMULAS AND VIEWS

If you still combine the points from the previous chapter with important behavioral views and question some of your own rules, nothing will stand in the way of your personal wealth. For this purpose, the following questions/points should be critically considered and, if necessary, realigned:

Are you rather going "towards something" or "away from something"?

In my opinion, the motivation to move towards something is always stronger than to move away from something. I like to ask this question in job interviews and actually expect the applicant to answer that the advertised position fits well with his profile and that he sees the position as a challenge or as a further development. Often enough, however, I hear as an answer that the applicant wants to leave his current company and position because ..., which is not a convincing motivation for me.

Do you follow an internal or external frame of reference?
Have you ever asked yourself what success is for you? You may be following your parents', friends' or society's definition of success. Success may be defined differently for you. If you have thought about it, are clearly sorted and act accordingly, you follow your inner

frame of reference, otherwise you follow an outer frame of reference.

In this context, I would also like to briefly address the topic of appreciation, which many people miss so much (from others). From my point of view, you should first manage to give yourself the necessary appreciation (inner frame of reference). In addition: Do you show the necessary appreciation to all the people around you? Moreover, by that I really mean everyone. Pretty hard, isn't it? One immediately thinks of the boss, the mother-in-law, the brother, the sister, with whom one has perhaps been at loggerheads for some time. Moreover, I am supposed to show them appreciation. After they have treated me like this. Quite simply: Yes, you should! If you do not feel appreciation towards these people, how can you feel appreciation for yourself? You also make mistakes or you are not satisfied with every of your actions in retrospect. In addition, you do not know whether one of these persons is possibly your ass angel, as Robert Betz describes it so beautifully in his books. You can mirror yourself particularly well on these people, because they push buttons with you that make your adrenaline level rise particularly and you should find out why this is so. For me, this is also part of the further development of your own behavior.

Do you tend to perceive your own needs or those of others?
Do you often want to "please others"? Why is that? Are you looking for recognition or appreciation? When was the last time you asked yourself what your needs are? If you try to please everyone, you will end up pleasing no

one.

Do you perceive similarities or differences?
Honestly, when you compare yourself to others, do you notice the similarities or the differences? Yes, it was similar for me: we first look at what makes us different. We owe that to our ego. To be successful, however, we should pay more attention to how our behavior resembles that of successful people.

What is your personal persuasion strategy?
How do you convince others of your views / your opinion? How do you form your opinion? Do you listen carefully to other people? Do you watch a lot of news or read many magazines? Do you read many books or do you work with others in a team? After you have formed an opinion, how do you convince your counterpart? Do you repeat your views, possibly over a longer period? Alternatively, is a one-time but clear statement enough for you?

Do you rather perceive opportunities or necessities?
How many good opportunities have you missed? I have been abroad twice with my family on business because the opportunity/opportunity arose. I grabbed it, although the transfer abroad with children in luggage turned out to be not so easy. Many colleagues told me that they would do the same if the opportunity arose. However, if you look more closely, the opportunities were already there for them as well. They were just not being used. Why not? Now I would have to jump back to the chapter on "feeling safe". I think that for most people, such a step is too uncertain and risky.

Do you work more independently or cooperatively?
How would you describe your work style? Do you like to work alone or with others in a team? What is a team for you? Do you live the thought: "Great someone else will do it" - or do you rise to the task? This question is important whether you work in a team or alone. If you face the task, then the question is how? Half-heartedly or with full commitment? Your life should be a "full throttle" event. That is, when you do something, please do it with full dedication or do not do it at all.

AFTERWORD

Dear Reader,

With this book, I hope I have brought you closer to my personal approach regarding the connection between spiritual thinking and personal wealth.

Many questions have been asked and this book has answered certainly not all of them. Some answers you should find out for yourself.

In my opinion, you can achieve wealth primarily through permanent personal development and a changed approach to thinking. Material wealth arises almost inevitably from this.

The self-confident attainment of personal freedom is achieved through self-love, present-mindedness and unambiguous action. Fearlessness and an inner compass let success models develop over courageous decisions.

I hope that my elaborations will give rise to new thoughts in you, which will lead you in new directions. Wealth comes mainly through change. Through change of yourself and the peeling out of your real self.

Now go out and implement the parts of it that have particularly appealed to you, if that is what you really want. Change yourself and you will feel the development of your wealth.

In addition, remember Albert Schweitzer's saying: "The greatest decision of your life lies in the fact that you can change your life by changing your mindset".

More quotes on the topics addressed, which were not discussed in the book text, but are apt:

> ➤ A man's wealth can be measured by the things he can do without, without losing his good humor.
> Henry David Thoreau (1817 - 1862), US.
> Philosopher, naturalist, writer and mystic

> ➤ Every encounter is an experience
> and every letting go is a realization.
> Unknown

> ➤ Letting go is silver, serenity is gold.
> Ernst Reinhardt (*1932)

> ➤ Whoever tackles letting go has his hands full.
> Almut Adler (*1951)

> ➤ Egoism arises from a lack of self-love.
> Andreas Tenzer (*1954)

> ➤ Self-love makes us completely what we are.
> Claude-Adrien Helvetius (1715 - 1771)

> ➤ Consciousness is perception of the nothingness of being-there.
> Michael Wollmann (*1990)

> ➤ Nothing will change as long as we do not change.
> Justus Vogt (*1958)

- ➢ Have courage for courage, instead of fear of fear.
  Antje Schulz (*1972)

- ➢ Freedom is the possibility to realize one's own goals.
  Unknown

- ➢ Success is the achievement of self-determined goals.
  Manfred Helfrecht (*1936)

- ➢ There is no such thing as certainty.
  Erwin Koch (*1932)

- ➢ The search for security is an illusion.
  Unknown

- ➢ Life can never offer security, only chances.
  Unknown

- ➢ Security and freedom - rarely available as a set.
  Esther Klepgen (*1965)

Here is a list of the underlying and further literature on the book topic that motivated me to write this book:

- Anthony Robbins: Limitless Energy - The Power Principle.
  This book is about overcoming blockages and fears in life and how one can successfully manage any situation with the right communication with one's own subconscious and achieve success results.

- Christian Bischoff: Consciousness
  In order to control thoughts and feelings in such a way that we act and live as we want, the existence of awareness is of paramount importance.

- Diana Cooper: I give myself a new life - Seven steps to myself
  To change one's life, improve relationships and health, ideas for inner transformation are given here in steps.

- Don Miguel Ruiz: The Four Promises - A Path to Freedom and Dignity.
  The realization of the dream of freedom, joy and love comes through the liberation of the nightmare of fear, abuse and violence.

- Don Miguel Ruiz/Don Jose Ruiz: The Fifth Promise
  Be skeptical, but listen carefully.

- Eckhart Tolle: A New Earth - Leap of

Consciousness Instead of Self-Destruction
The book is a tool of transformation. It contains signposts that point to awakening.

- Eckhart Tolle: Now! The power of the present
An epoch-making work. "The worst thing that can happen to you (while reading this book) is that you look into a mirror where you expect to see your little self, and find that your true self is looking back at you."(Vera Birkenbihl)

- Harald Wessbecher: Unfold your destiny - Live as it suits and pleases you.
Everyone has a life task; everyone has a very personal destiny. Recognizing and fulfilling it leads to freedom and true happiness.

- Michael A. Singer: The Experiment of Devotion - My Path to the Perfection of Life
A narrative of the path to the perfection of life. Autobiography of a yogi who is fully engaged in the world.

- Osho: Consciousness - Observe without judging
Only when we are awake are all the faculties of our consciousness available to us. This leads to true freedom and mastery of life.

- Osho: The Book of the Ego - From the Illusion of the Ego to the Freedom of Being
Through our ego, a false self is built up. Liberation can be achieved through meditation, awareness and love.

- Osho: Courage - Live wild and dangerous
  To confront one's fears in full awareness means courage and the willingness to face the fundamental uncertainty of life.

- Robert Betz: Out of the old shoes!
  Decluttering one's life can be done by removing inhibitions such as self-judgment, dwelling on the past, and the need for perfection.

- Ryan Holiday: Your Ego is Your Enemy - How to Defeat Your Biggest Enemy
  Many people believe that the reasons that prevent them from being successful are found in their environment. In reality, the biggest enemy is within each of us: our ego. It blinds us to our mistakes, prevents us from learning from them and hinders our development.

- Theo Fisher: Maturity - the key to happiness
  In order to understand one's life and no longer be tied down in prejudices, emotional dependencies and compulsions to conform, one must develop maturity.

ABOUT THE AUTHOR

Richard Schleinkofer, born on 30.11.1967, businessperson and father of three children, has made it his concern to connect spiritual ways of thinking with personal and economic success. He lived and worked with his family in Greece for a total of five years. On numerous trips abroad, he had the opportunity to get to know the different cultural perspectives on this subject.